4TH GRADE PHONICS READING PASSAGES
Comprehension Questions and Word Work

Read the passage two times. Then circle words with: -le, ch, soft c

A Bunch of Toppings

Shiloh was busy making an ice cream
chose vanilla ice cream as the base b
she wanted to add a bunch of toppin
hard to decide which topping to sta
Shiloh was ready to begin. First, Sh
up some strawberries. She placed
the ice cream. Then, Shiloh shook
over the vanilla ice cream. Last, S
to drizzle chocolate sauce on top
chocolate sauce dripped down ir
Shiloh traced one of the curly b
finger, to try a sample. Her ice
now had plenty of toppings, wh
one thing. It was time to gobb

© Literacy with Aylin Claahsen 2024- present

Write words from the story: **A Bunch of Toppings**

-le	ch	soft c

Answer the questions:

1. Why did Shiloh choose vanilla ice cream as the base?

2. What did Shiloh do with the chopped up strawberries?

3. Which topping did she decide to add second?

4. Which topping did she trace with her finger to have a taste?

© Literacy with Aylin Claahsen 2024- present. All rights reserved

Table of Contents	Page
A Bunch of Toppings	6-7
The Relay Race	8-9
The Reader	10-11
Support	12-13
The Worst Slice	14-15
Switching Gears	16-17
Too Tired	18-19
A Discount	20-21
The Actor	22-23
Impossible	24-25
Remix	26-27
New Positions	28-29
A Bigger Smudge	30-31
Wilbur	32-33
A Coastal Setting	34-35
Focus Words Answer Key	37-39
Answer Keys for Questions	41-43

Instructions for Use

The main purpose of this pack is to help students develop their reading skills. They will read grade level appropriate words, work on fluency with repeated readings, and also work on comprehension by writing responses to the comprehension questions for each passage.

Each Passage:
The student will read each passage two times. After reading the text a second time, the student will highlight or circle words that match the focus concepts listed at the top of each passage.

Focus Words List:
Students will then choose three words to list for each focus pattern, on the next page, before answering the comprehension questions.

Comprehension Questions:
Each passage comes with its own set of comprehension questions. After the student has read through the text two times, they can write their answers to the comprehension questions.

Answer Keys:
Two different Answer Keys are provided at the end of this workbook. One set includes all the focus words that students may have selected for each passages. The second set includes answers for the comprehension questions. You can use both of these answer keys to check the student's responses.

A Bunch of Toppings

Shiloh was busy making an ice cream cone. She chose vanilla ice cream as the base because she wanted to add a bunch of toppings. It was hard to decide which topping to start with, but Shiloh was ready to begin. First, Shiloh chopped up some strawberries. She placed them all over the ice cream. Then, Shiloh shook sprinkles all over the vanilla ice cream. Last, Shiloh decided to drizzle chocolate sauce on top. The chocolate sauce dripped down in squiggles. Shiloh traced one of the curly lines with her finger, to try a sample. Her ice cream cone now had plenty of toppings, which meant only one thing. It was time to gobble it all up!

-le

ch

soft c

Answer the questions:

1. Why did Shiloh choose vanilla ice cream as the base?

_____

_____

2. What did Shiloh do with the chopped up strawberries?

_____

_____

3. Which topping did she decide to add second?

_____

_____

4. Which topping did she trace with her finger to have a taste?

_____

_____

The Relay Race

Maxwell could be easily swayed. He often switched his mind when making a choice. Sid needed one more fast kid on his team, so that his team of four could win the relay race. Sid knew he'd be able to change Maxwell's mind. He just had to approach him calmly. Otherwise, Maxwell would know something was up. Sid walked up to Maxwell and started out with a friendly conversation. After some small talk, Sid brought up the topic of Maxwell joining his relay team. Sid explained that they just needed one more _really_ fast kid. Maxwell began smiling, and so did Sid. He knew Maxwell was willing to join his team. They walked to the starting line together. They couldn't wait to win the race!

Write words from the story: **The Relay Race**

-ly	compound words	-all/-alk
_____	_____	_____
_____	_____	_____
_____	_____	_____

Answer the questions:

1. What was Sid's strategy to get Maxwell to join the relay team?

_____

_____

2. How did Sid begin the conversation with Maxwell?

_____

_____

3. How do you know Sid's strategy worked?

_____

_____

4. Why did Maxwell begin smiling when Sid mentioned he needed just "one more really fast kid" in the race?

_____

_____

The Reader

Harper was randomly chosen to be the reader for the day, meaning she was in charge of reading the directions on the page, to her whole class. Harper didn't like being a speaker. It was a big challenge for her to feel brave when she spoke aloud. She didn't mind reading, but reading aloud was not something she enjoyed. Harper slouched down in her chair. She hoped her teacher would just skip to another kid. Then her teacher crouched down next to her and started whispering very softly. Hearing her teacher's kind words, Harper grinned and felt more confident. Harper was ready to tackle the directions. She quickly read them aloud and then looked up to see her classmates giving her thumbs up for a job well done!

Write words from the story:

-er (Latin suffix)	-ou	ch-
_____	_____	_____
_____	_____	_____
_____	_____	_____

Answer the questions:

1. What did it mean to be the "reader for the day"?

_____

2. How must have Harper felt when she was chosen to be the reader for the day? How do you know?

_____

3. What did Harper do in her chair when it was her turn?

_____

4. When Harper read the directions, how did she know she did a good job reading aloud?

_____

Support

We got to the airport right on time. My family was on our way to a resort on the beach. The flight would be slightly longer than we were used to. We were flying to a different country. I'd watched my dad check his backpack for our passports at least twelve times. He was clearly rather overwhelmed about the travel plans. I didn't want him becoming any more stressed out, so I offered my support. I suggested we go grab his favorite snack and sit and watch the airplanes take off. Once we grabbed the snacks, and sat down by the windows, he seemed to be less stressed. The snack had done the trick in taking the edge off. I was pleased with myself for being supportive!

Write words from the story:		Support

-or	-ea	-igh
_____	_____	_____
_____	_____	_____
_____	_____	_____

Answer the questions:

1. Where was the family headed?

_____

_____

2. Why do you think the dad was so stressed and overwhelmed?

_____

_____

3. How did his child offer support?

_____

_____

4. How did the snack help the dad become less overwhelmed?

_____

_____

The Worst Slice

Alonso was disgusted and felt sick to his stomach. That was the grossest slice of pizza he'd ever tried. He discarded his plate into the nearest trash can, as soon as possible. Alonso started the slowest walk ever home from the pizza place. While he walked, he tried to stop thinking about the pizza. But he was in disbelief with how terrible it tasted. When he got home, Alonso told his brother about the pizza that was so horrible. His brother asked what was on the pizza. His brother started laughing when Alonso described the tiny fish that was on his slice. His brother then explained that he'd tried that type of pizza before too. He also thought it was the worst kind of pizza.

Write words from the story:		The Worst Slice

dis-	-est	-ible

Answer the questions:

1. Why do you think Alonso walked home slowly from the pizza place?

_____

_____

2. As Alonso walked, what did he try to stop doing?

_____

_____

3. Why did Alonso's brother laugh when Alonso revealed to him what was on his pizza slice?

_____

_____

4. Do you think Alonso will try that pizza again? Why or why not?

_____

_____

Switching Gears

My sister Quinn was right a lot, but not always. Today, she was incorrect, but she wouldn't budge. Quinn always felt like she had to be right. It drove me crazy. Today more so than ever, she kept driving me insane. She would not stop badgering me with the details of the topic. Most of the time, I just let her keep talking. But today, I couldn't stand it any longer. I tried to provide her with some insight explaining how she was wrong. However, she suddenly totally switched gears. Quinn dodged the subject by quickly talking about something new. It made me happy, for two reasons. First, her switching topics meant she actually knew she was wrong. Secondly, I no longer had to hear her go on and on!

Write words from the story:		Switching Gears

in-	-dge	-ly
_____	_____	_____
_____	_____	_____
_____	_____	_____

Answer the questions:

1. What would Quinn never admit?

_____

_____

2. What was driving Quinn's sister insane?

_____

_____

3. How did Quinn's sister explain that she was wrong?

_____

_____

4. What were the two reasons Quinn's sister was happy, at the end of the story?

_____

_____

Too Tired

Unpacking the car was taking forever and Carlos was already half asleep. It had been a long drive and he just wanted to sleep. Carlos unrolled his sleeping bag and started to climb in. The sleeping bag was too tight, so he climbed back out. He then unzipped the sleeping bag from top to bottom. Carlos fell asleep right away, but woke up with numb fingers. He got a hold of his bag and tried to unzip it, but his thumbs weren't working. They were so numb he couldn't get them to grasp the zipper. Too tired to try again, Carlos shoved his hands in his pockets and fell back asleep. He smiled when he woke up to the sun shining into his tent. Carlos was also happy to feel his hands again. Time to start the day!

Write words from the story:		Too Tired

un-	-mb	-er (r controlled vowel)
_____	_____	_____
_____	_____	_____
_____	_____	_____

Answer the questions:

1. What was the first thing Carlos did when he got out of the car?

_____

_____

2. What was wrong with the sleeping bag when Carlos first climbed in?

_____

_____

3. Why couldn't Carlos get a hold of the sleeping bag's zipper?

_____

_____

4. When Carlos woke up, what were two things that made him happy?

_____

_____

A Discount

This warehouse was huge with rows of giant shelves. Everywhere I looked I saw something that I wanted to purchase. I walked up and down the rows with my dad by my side. Each time I showed him something I wanted, he told me to keep looking. It was hard to pick just one thing, but I made a choice. I ended up choosing a chapter book, that was on sale. I also got an extra discount on the book, since I was a student. I was pleased with my purchase and the price I paid. Even with so many things to choose from, I only picked one thing that would make me the happiest. I knew my dad was proud of me since I didn't overspend. Plus, I think he was looking forward to reading the book with me!

-ar/-or/-ur	-ou	soft c/g
_____	_____	_____
_____	_____	_____
_____	_____	_____

Answer the questions:

1. What did the narrator find difficult about his experience at the large store?

_____

_____

2. Why was the narrator happy about his decision to choose a chapter book?

_____

_____

3. Why was his dad proud of him?

_____

_____

4. What is the narrator looking forward to with his chapter book?

_____

_____

The Actor

The actor walked out onto the stage. Everyone gasped as he switched from role to role. He was a one man show and everyone was blown away. Ivy sat at the edge of her seat. She couldn't wait to see what the actor would do next. Ivy stretched her neck to peek at the director who was watching from backstage. The director had a big grin on her face. She was clearly happy that the actor was doing such a wonderful job. As a visitor of the theater, Ivy was also thrilled. This was the first time she'd been up close to an expert actor. Ivy knew that the visit to the theater was ending with a chance to act with this actor. She was going to soak up everything she could from this visit!

-or (Latin suffix)   -tch   soft c/g

_____	_____	_____
_____	_____	_____
_____	_____	_____

Answer the questions:

1. How could you tell that the actor was talented?

_____

_____

2. What did Ivy notice about the director?

_____

_____

3. Why was Ivy looking forward to the end of the show?

_____

_____

4. How can you tell Ivy enjoyed being a visitor at this theater?

_____

_____

Impossible

Jaden's baby sister was adorable. Camila liked to do everything Jaden did. Jaden could admit that it was enjoyable to have someone who always wanted to be by your side. But sometimes Jaden didn't want Camila to follow him. Today was one of those days because he just wanted to play with his friends, by himself. However, when Camila grabbed his hand with her sticky little fingers, Jaden knew it was hopeless. He couldn't go outside without her, so he scooped her up and gave her a smooch. Camila smiled at Jaden and squeezed him tightly, in a warm hug. It was as if Camila knew that she was just so lovable. Jaden knew she was harmless and wouldn't ruin his day with his friends anyway. They trooped outside together. It was just worthless to try and do anything without her!

Write words from the story:		**Impossible**
-able (Latin suffix)	-less	-oo
_____ _____	_____ _____	_____ _____

Answer the questions:

1. Why didn't Jaden want Camila to play with him that day?

_____

2. When Camila grabbed Jaden's hand, what did he do?

_____

3. How did Jaden know Camila wouldn't ruin the day with his friends?

_____

4. When Jaden decided that Camila could come, what did they do together?

_____

Remix

My dad loves to remix songs. He can take any song and replace the words with new ones to fit whatever we are doing. My dad always gets so into it, as if he thinks he's in an audition to become the champion of a singing contest. His upbeat songs make me giggle, most of the time. I refrain from laughing when his remix is addressing something I refuse to do. However, even then, I don't withhold my laughter for long. His singing usually derails me from what I'm refusing to do. It almost always works to get me to follow through on my obligation. It's mainly because I don't want to hear him sing about the situation for an extended time. My dad also remixes songs during a celebration. At those times I usually smile, right away. His dedication to each remix is priceless!

Write words from the story: **Remix**

re-	-ion/-tion	-ai
_____	_____	_____
_____	_____	_____
_____	_____	_____

Answer the questions:

1. When his dad gets into a song he's remixing, what is it like?

_____

_____

2. When does he refrain from laughing at his dad?

_____

_____

3. What is an "obligation"?

_____

_____

4. When does the narrator smile right away at his dad's remixes?

_____

_____

New Positions

The players gathered on the field to hear their new roles for the game. It seemed risky to put players in brand new positions, but they trusted their coach. Peyton found out she was the catcher, while Ella was the pitcher. Once the batter approached the mound, the umpire nodded to Ella. It was her signal to begin. Ella frowned as she looked down at her sweating hands. Then she looked up and saw Peyton looking directly at her. Peyton's face was intense, but warm at the same time. It was clear Peyton believed in Ella's pitching. Ella suddenly felt confident. She pitched the ball which landed right in Peyton's glove. The batter had swung and missed. Ella instantly felt relief. Maybe this new position would be doable!

Write words from the story:		New Positions
-er (Latin suffix)	-ou/-ow	-ie

Answer the questions:

1. When the players gathered on the field, what seemed risky to them?

_____

_____

2. How can you tell Ella felt nervous on the mound?

_____

_____

3. What made Ella believe in herself?

_____

_____

4. What happened when Ella pitched the ball?

_____

_____

A Bigger Smudge

Nori did not budge from her seat. She watched as the fudge melted in her hands, right onto her brand new white dress. Fearful of how her mom would react, Nori tried to think fast. Barely moving, Nori placed the melting fudge down on the table. Secretly, she then swiped a wipe from her mom's purse. Nori quickly, but in a careful manner, wiped at the stain on her dress. Dread came over her as she watched the fudge seep deeper into the dress. The small stain was now a bigger smudge. Wishing she could flee from the shop, she knew she had to show her mom the damage. Nori's mom surprisingly didn't get mad. She grabbed something that looked like a pen from her purse and rubbed it directly on the stain. Her mom's carefree response shocked Nori, but it also made her feel so much better!

-dge	-ly	-ee
_____	_____	_____
_____	_____	_____
_____	_____	_____

Answer the questions:

1. What landed on Nori's dress?

_____

_____

2. What was Nori's solution to the stain?

_____

_____

3. What happened when Nori tried to wipe the fudge from her dress?

_____

_____

4. What surprised Nori?

_____

_____

Wilbur

Abdul and Nazeer's pet gerbil, named Wilbur, had disappeared. They both blamed each other and disagreed about the last location Wilbur had been. Abdul was convinced that Nazeer had Wilbur in his room while Abdul was in the kitchen. Nazeer thought Abdul left Wilbur down in the basement. They both were disappointed and knew they had to locate Wilbur soon. Abdul and Nazeer recognized they weren't accomplishing anything by being angry. They were simply being wasteful with their time. They knew if they merged their memories together, it would be helpful in finding Wilbur. Abdul and Nazeer sat down and started making a list of where they'd been that day. They pinpointed a spot they hadn't talked about yet. Feeling hopeful, they ran to the family room. Their merging of memories had worked, Wilbur was sitting right on the couch!

Write words from the story: **Wilbur**

-ful	dis-	soft c/g
_____	_____	_____
_____	_____	_____

Answer the questions:

1. What happened to Wilbur?

_____

2. How were Abdul and Nazeer being wasteful with their time?

_____

3. What did Abdul and Nazeer do to merge their memories together?

_____

4. In which room were they hopeful to find Wilbur?

_____

A Coastal Setting

On a normal day, Baxter loved being by my side all day long. But today, he was so gloomy. I tried to snuggle Baxter, and nuzzle my face in his furry neck. But he instantly got off the couch and sat down in his crate. I sat next to Baxter and tried to tickle him behind his ears. That always made him happy, except for today. He spun around so that he was no longer looking my direction. As I stared outside at the snowstorm, I realized his gloominess might be a reaction to the bitter cold. Winter was just not his favorite season since he couldn't be outside as much. This was clearly a seasonal problem. I needed to get crafty to uplift his mood. I made a warm coastal setting in my room where the sun was shining in. I coaxed him to that spot and fed him dog cookies from the local pet bakery. That seemed to do the trick which uplifted both our moods!

Write words from the story: **A Coastal Setting**

-al

-y (long e sound)

-le

_____

_____

_____

_____

_____

_____

Answer the questions:

1. What did Baxter normally love to do?

_____

_____

2. What did Baxter's owner do to try and make him feel better?

_____

_____

3. What did his owner realize was making Baxter so gloomy?

_____

_____

4. What did Baxter's owner do to make him feel less gloomy?

_____

_____

Focus Words Answer Key:

You can use these to check the focus words listed for each passage.

Story Title	Focus 1	Focus 2	Focus 3
A Bunch of Toppings	-le: drizzle squiggles sprinkles gobble sample	ch: chose Bunch which chopped chocolate	soft c: ice placed decided sauce traced
The Relay Race	-ly: easily calmly friendly really	compound words: Maxwell something otherwise	-all/-alk: small walked talk
The Reader	-er (Latin suffix meaning person connected with): reader speaker teacher	-ou: aloud slouched crouched	ch-: chosen charge challenge chair
Support	-or (r controlled vowel): airport resort support passports	-ea: beach least clearly pleased	-igh: right flight slightly
The Worst Slice	dis-: disgusted discarded disbelief	-est (comparative ending): grossest nearest slowest	-ible (Latin suffix meaning can be done): terrible possible horrible

Focus Words Answer Key:

You can use these to check the focus words listed for each passage.

Story Title	Focus 1	Focus 2	Focus 3
Switching Gears	in-: incorrect insane insight	-dge: budge badgering dodged	-ly: suddenly totally actually quickly secondly
Too Tired	un-: unpacking unrolled unzipped	-mb: climb numb thumbs	-er (r controlled vowel): forever fingers zipper
A Discount	-ar/-ur/-or: hard forward purchase	-ou: warehouse discount proud	soft c/g: huge giant choice since price
The Actor	-or (Latin suffix meaning person connected with): actor director visitor	-tch: switched stretched watching	soft c/g: face chance stage edge
Impossible	-able (Latin suffix meaning can be done): adorable enjoyable lovable	-less: hopeless harmless worthless	-oo: scooped smooch trooped

Focus Words Answer Key:

You can use these to check the focus words listed for each passage.

Story Title	Focus 1	Focus 2	Focus 3
Remix	re-: remix replace refuse	-ion/-tion: audition champion obligation situation celebration dedication	-ai: refrain derails mainly
New Positions	-er (Latin suffix meaning person connected with): players catcher pitcher batter	-ou/-ow: found out mound frowned down	-ie: field relief believed
A Bigger Smudge	-dge: budge smudge fudge	-ly: barely secretly quickly surprisingly directly	-ee: seep deeper carefree flee feel
Wilbur	-ful: wasteful helpful hopeful	dis-: disappeared disagreed disappointed	soft c/soft g: convinced gerbil merged merging
A Coastal Setting	-al: normal seasonal coastal local	-y (long e sound): gloomy furry happy crafty	-le: snuggle nuzzle tickle

Answer Key

You can use these to check the written answers to each comprehension question.

Story Title	Question 1	Question 2	Question 3	Question 4
A Bunch of Toppings	She chose vanilla ice cream because she wanted to add a bunch of toppings.	Shiloh placed the strawberries all over the ice cream.	Shiloh added sprinkles to her ice cream second.	Shiloh traced the chocolate drizzle for a quick sample.
The Relay Race	Sid's strategy was to approach him calmly, so that he wouldn't know anything was up.	He started out with friendly conversation.	His strategy worked because Maxwell ended up running in the race as his teammate.	Maxwell began smiling because he was receiving a compliment.
The Reader	Being the reader for the day meant that Harper had to read the directions aloud to her class.	Harper must have felt shy when she was chosen to be the reader because she didn't like being a speaker.	Harper slouched down in her chair.	Harper knew she did a good job reading aloud because her classmates gave her thumbs up.
Support	The family was headed to a resort on the beach.	The dad was so stressed because they were going to a different country and was worried about the passports.	His child offered support by suggesting to watch planes and eat his favorite snack.	The snack helped the dad feel less stressed about the flight by taking the edge off.
The Worst Slice	He walked slowly because he felt terrible and was disgusted by the pizza.	He tried to stop thinking about the horrible pizza.	His brother laughed because he too has had that kind of terrible pizza before and thought it was the grossest kind.	Alonso will not try that pizza again because the text said he was, "...disgusted and felt sick..."

Answer Key

You can use these to check the written answers to each comprehension question.

Story Title	Question 1	Question 2	Question 3	Question 4
Switching Gears	Quinn would never admit when she was incorrect.	Quinn's sister was going insane because Quinn would not stop badgering about a certain topic.	Quinn's sister explained that she was incorrect by providing some insight instead of letting her talk on and on.	First, Quinn realized she was incorrect. Second, Quinn's sister could sit in silence and not have to hear her sister's badgering.
Too Tired	Carlos unrolled his sleeping bag and climbed in.	When he first climbed in, the sleeping bag was too tight.	He couldn't grab the zipper because his fingers were too numb and his thumbs weren't working properly.	Carlos was happy because the sun was shining and he could feel his fingers.
A Discount	He found it hard to pick just one thing he wanted – and only one thing.	He was happy because the chapter book was discounted and he felt content with the price he paid.	His dad was proud of this purchase because his child didn't overspend.	He's looking forward to reading the book with his dad.
The Actor	The actor was talented because everyone was blown away as he switched roles.	The director was impressed and happy that the actor was doing well.	At the end of the show, there was a chance to act on stage with the actor.	Ivy enjoyed being a visitor at the theater because it says she was "thrilled."
Impossible	Jaden just wanted to play with his friends by himself.	Jaden scooped her up and gave her a smooch.	Camila was always harmless and adorable.	They trooped outside to enjoy the day.

Answer Key

You can use these to check the written answers to each comprehension question.

Story Title	Question 1	Question 2	Question 3	Question 4
Remix	It's as if his dad is becoming the champion of a singing contest.	The narrator refrains from laughing at his dad when the remix is addressing something he refuses to do.	An obligation is something you have to do.	The narrator smiles when his dad remixes at a celebration.
New Positions	It seemed risky to put players in new positions on the field that they've never played before.	When Ella was on the mound, she looked down at "her sweating hands" and she "frowned."	Peyton's intense but warm face made Ella believe that she could do it.	The ball landed right in Peyton's glove!
A Bigger Smudge	Melting fudge landed on her dress and made a smudge.	Her solution was to quickly grab a wipe from her mom's purse to wipe up the fudge.	The smudge got bigger and seeped deeper into the dress.	Nori was surprised that her mom didn't get upset and was carefree about the smudge.
Wilbur	Wilbur disappeared.	They were being wasteful by arguing and blaming each other.	They created a list of where they had been that day.	They were hopeful that Wilbur was in the family room.
A Costal Setting	Baxter normally enjoyed being by his owner's side.	He tried to snuggle Baxter and nuzzle into his neck. He also tried to tickle him behind the ears.	Baxter was gloomy because of the snowstorm and cold.	His owner created a coastal setting in a sunny spot in his room. He also grabbed some treats from the local bakery.

Terms of Use

This resource is for personal use/single classroom use only. Placing any part of this product on the Internet (including classroom, school or district websites) is prohibited by the Digital Millennium Copyright Act (DMCA).

literacywithaylinclaahsen.com

Scan the QR code to follow me on Instagram for more ideas!

Made in United States
Orlando, FL
16 March 2025

59530062R00026